A SAFE HOUSE

Christa Wells

ISBN-979-8-218-31676-1

Cover Photograph by Christa Wells

Book Cover and Typesetting by MarzArts

For Mom and Dad,
who have welcomed so many
into the safe arms of their love

Art by Shelly Eve | shellyeve.com

Contents

Preface...7

Never Dreamed I Would......................................9

Black-Eyed Susans 10

Rental House..11

Reforestation 12

Parts...13

Devotion 15

Talking Myself Out Of Giving Up.....................16

Invisible..17

Ghost Story 18

Greenhouse Blues 19

Holy Matrimony 20

Seed Catcher 21

The Introvert...22

Growth...23

Army Brat, Thirty Years On 24

At Home In The World......................................25

This Is Not The Poem That Will Change Your Life............26

Creator's Prayer...27

Piano Keys..28

Where To Begin...29

What The Soul Wants..30

Vows 32

I Am The House 33

Why It Happened...34

Lullaby...35

My Boy 36

Howard And Wilma 37

Old Friend 38

Between Us.. 39

On Your Birthday 40

What She Remembers.. 41

Growing Years 42

From This Day Forward.. 43

Renaissance 44

Daughter 45

Annual Performance 46

No One Tells Us 47

I Keep Coming Back.. 48

In The Field Beyond The House................................ 49

Provocateur 50

Land Of The Living 51

Nothing Shall Be Impossible.................................... 52

I'm Praying Again, Aren't I?...................................... 53

The End Of Suffering 54

To Leave Behind A Critical Heart.............................. 55

Disarming 56

I've Heard It Said.. 57

Three Portals 58

Life Itself 59

Disciple 60

A Safe House 61

PREFACE

The pattern is clear: an idea arrives, I wait five minutes and then step right out onto some virtual balcony to announce what I'll be making next. It doesn't seem to matter how many people hear the announcement; more than accountability, it's the connection I feel to you who sit across from me as I write, receiving my voice into the rooms of your world. You are my quiet collaborator, companion and motivation to see the thing through.

Everything changed for me in 2017 when my marriage ended, but change is the gold thread that runs through the fabric of all our lives. I was changed again when I shared my first collection of poems, **BELOVED**, three years into my healing process. It became another example of sharing before I felt fully ready or expert or qualified–and seeing the work bear good fruit anyway.

So here I am three years farther on, offering a second collection of poems. *A SAFE HOUSE* wades in the waters of relationship–with self, the other, nature and the divine. The theme of "safety"--how, where and why we seek or create it for ourselves and each other–runs throughout.

My intent is to give readers a fresh spark of desire to transform the world we share–and ourselves–into safe houses, where we are able to be our truest selves and share peace. Thank you for being such a place for me.

Christa
November 8, 2023

NEVER DREAMED I WOULD

bury what I buried
hurt as I hurt
rage as I raged
survive what I survived
forgive what I've forgiven
be held as I've been held
go where I've gone
find what I've found
create what I've created
love as I love
be who I've become.

BLACK-EYED SUSANS

Other hands can write
about divorce and what it takes from a person.
I wish to write about waking
this morning from a deep sleep
before the alarm sounded—

how cool it suddenly became
as I sipped coffee on the porch
and thumbed through poems
written centuries before I learned to read,
letting the old Persian pull me into his
ecstatic God-dance.

I can accept what happened while I tell you
how just this afternoon I was able to salvage
three whole vases of Black-Eyed Susans
from a single grocery store bouquet,
sorting the lifeless from the living.

I held them together, the bright and the brittle
before dropping the dead into the bin and turning
on the tap. Maybe we don't talk
about this enough, how something perfect
can expire and we still, with some help,
carry on blooming.

RENTAL HOUSE

Before we moved in, the owner painted
gray the floor of the porch–
layering paint over the old
so the soles of my feet
stand on craters of a flat silver moon,
outlines of the long ago
before us.

We landed here, the kids and I,
five years ago, in need of three bedrooms
and a bathroom, for a mother and her four,
sometimes five, teenagers.

Yesterday I discovered the remains
of a bird's nest atop the porch light.
Recycled weeds, green leaves,
bits of rope and puffs of fuzz,
a dropped veil of southern moss.

She must have moved in while I was working
or sleeping, designed a home for her brood
with treasures thrifted
from the local shops.

She must have understood
it does not have to be eternal
to be called good,
to be what you need it to be.

We do seem to find what we look for
piece by piece, packing our beaks,
whatever it takes really,
to keep the children alive.

REFORESTATION

After the war
we considered rebuilding.
Instead we planted a tree
in the crater heart of the wound.

It did not take one night but a thousand
for the roots to reach refuge
and a thousand more for limbs
to flower and fruit.

It didn't take one night but a thousand
for those branches to brim with moonlight,
and moonlight to summon songbirds,
lauding morning at midnight.

Lean on me, children,
while the dark dreams through
the nest, resting us together,
near peace.

PARTS

I'm riding
   the light
      down
into streets
where power's
gone
   out
      and forlorn
aspects of
   myself
      sit waiting
on curbs.

Children
   mostly
stuck in time,
on the days
      their fears
were founded
at home
   or on the playground,
silenced,
   humiliated
or left behind.

I am
on my way
to meet them
   one by one
slowly, unfold
and hold them
   if they allow me
to hold
their stories,

so they don't have to
anymore.

For all
our sakes,
I wish them
    relief.
May they be made safe
    with me,
safe to unclench
    the small fists
that have worked
so hard
to protect

    Us.

DEVOTION

The porch has grown cold in October.
A building rises precisely
where the sun sets each night.

Still I am hot with love
for this place I have been given
and won't give up so easily.

I devote my mouth to smiling
at the wolf spider spinning
her strange web for me.

I donate my heart to humanity
as hers is almost always broken.
What else have I got to give?

Why should I not commit
to the only home I've known,
doomed as it may be?

Why should I not move manic,
throwing my leaflets around
and telling everyone I meet

to save themselves, and now?
Haven't I seen enough to know
a whole heart can heal what ails
the body?

TALKING MYSELF OUT OF GIVING UP

Don't believe the stories
you hear–or the ones you tell–
about how awful everything
and everybody is.

After all, everytime I look
for someone good
or kind, I find them.
And what about that pink
lemonade sky that came cascading
into the bay last night?

Sometimes I fly away
only to return and find
the birdsong cinematic
at home as it was abroad.

It's only that I forget
to be astonished.

INVISIBLE

I'm sorry, Wheaton.
I'm sorry, Fairfax.
It wasn't you, after all.

I blamed your high schools
and pep rallies
the kids born rich
or blonde
with the posture
of the self-assured.

I made myself a vapor—
how could they not
walk through
me?

Resentment—mine—
spread like kudzu, erasing faces
leaving me alone
with the happy chatter
and the lying insider
trading on my inferiority
complex.

I can't tell you what they looked like,
those kids, what they loved
or dreamed of becoming,
not even a single one
of their names.

GHOST STORY

I remember saying,
I'm pretty sure my presence doesn't matter.

From childhood this one thought had me
peering up at giants.

Then lightning: It is precisely my presence,
presence and nothing else,

that sees and makes seen,
that pulls people from thin air.

Where have I been all these years?

GREENHOUSE BLUES

I am not skilled
with potted plants
but not yet done
with trying.

I have not sung
with my full voice
but every day
I open.

Water often
makes the difference—
soaked or dried out,
no safety.

The window, too,
with the correct
slant of sun—
this matters.

I'm so sorry,
I say again.
Keep forgetting
what you need.

HOLY MATRIMONY

There is a voice I would follow
to the ends of the earth,
a path that urges my fidelity.

I was once wed to the vows
I pledged when I was twenty,
committed to a course
that stretched many miles
farther than child-eyes could see.

Today I have married myself
to what cannot be outgrown
though dedication it does require.

Listening, you have my heart.
Morning. Noon. And night.

While eggs sizzle and coffee
is poured. While driving down Douglas
and waiting for the train to pass.
As my pen meets the page
and my heart starts,

yes, even now
waxing poetic
about this ecstatic love.
This late great love of my life.

Something speaks.
Something waits at the altar.
Something dearly beloved.

And I come running.

SEED CATCHER

How many of my sound ideas
find me in the shower
or meet me in the tree-lined tunnels
where the scent of pine
needles into the soft edges
of my awareness?

Each time is a near miss.
How close I come to canceling,
in light of the dentist appointment,
or the phone call,
or the empty refrigerator.

How close I come to being unavailable
for the conversation I came here to have!

So before work I remind myself:

Linger a little longer.
Sit naked in the steam.
Get dressed. Go outside. Walk around a while.

The seed opens in the soil
ready to receive.

THE INTROVERT

When night falls
without an invitation to
    decline,
smoke might slip inside
slither in through the cracks in my armor,
    an old loneliness
trying to get at me.
When that happens, I of course
make an escape.

But for now this gentle sunlight
    and my own generous company
convince me
canceled plans are a party
for one,
    such a dazzling delight
I smile without meaning to
and flutter my lashes.

I've nowhere to go

> *How delightful!*
> *How rare!*

And no idea
where to begin.

GROWTH

The crickets have changed their tune
and the sky has gone gray
without a whimper from me.

It's a sign, don't you think?

ARMY BRAT, THIRTY YEARS ON

Here is my room
with a desk and my bed
in the house I now call home.

This is my street
and my neighbors on porch chairs
waving back in the morning.

This is my city
and these are my people
who tell me they're glad I'm here.

This is me
tasting belonging
and leaving it on my tongue.

AT HOME IN THE WORLD

I like the way I walk now
into the shop
or crossing the lot.

Not like before
when I cast my eyes about
or tucked my chin and raised
my shoulders.

The movie that once played
in the background of my mind
has stopped.

There is no soundtrack to direct
my pace or posture.

This world–as it is–belongs to me.
I–as I am–belong to her,
for a little while.

It feels good not to be afraid
to be seen
together.

THIS IS NOT THE POEM THAT WILL CHANGE YOUR LIFE

but the one that pulls the chair
      out from under you

so you may stand up
and change it

yourself.

CREATOR'S PRAYER

If I cannot be the best
let me be among the first
to offer myself
to the work of being
what I am and nothing less.

I am willing, Love,
to be seen losing
myself in what is unseen,

to be caught trying,
to be known for spending my days making
something of my
confusion,

of the nothingness
I strive
to become.

May I lay aside
my desire for praise
and fill the wells of drought
with divine light.

PIANO KEYS

Watch out.

A soft flame
of afternoon light
might ignite the dust,

set the piano ablaze
and take you with it,

if you aren't careful
to keep yourself
in the dark

about what you really
want.

WHERE TO BEGIN

Tell the truth.
Get the guts on paper.

This is the first task,
and the hardest.

Many have an eye
for design.

How many willing
to center the soul?

WHAT THE SOUL WANTS

to opt out of the game
you never wanted to play

to bite hard on the thrown bone
and never return it

to lick the salt off your own wrist
and call it good

to be your own witness
when no one else steps forward
trusting there will be other days,
different, and crowded with life

to send up the guttural cry
locked so long inside
and hear it age into laughter

to pluck out your eyes,
soak them in vinegar 'til the lenses
come clean—
and see again, the world
in your arms

to walk away from weighted shapes
that feign finality,
and into luminous alleyways
of talking trees,
seeing yourself
as a greening part
of ancient branches

and your veined fingers
playing your grandmother's piano,
while you sing
for the simple pleasure
of kissing strangers
awake.

VOWS

What I sang
the morning of my marriage:

> If I can be anything
> –anything–
> I'll be yours.

At the age of twenty
I didn't know:

Before I am yours
I must always be
mine.

I AM THE HOUSE

I dreamed you came back.
We were natural, wordless.

It fell to me, of course,
to open the door and let you in.

Only then did I realize
I am not a person
with my hand on the knob.

Neither am I perched on a chair
in a state of wait.

I woke knowing:

I am the warmth of the kitchen in winter.
I am the table packed with chairs.
I am the roof that foils the rain
and the porch that offers shade.

I am the house
I am the house
I am the whole damn house.

The house that stays standing
after the guest
has gone away.

WHY IT HAPPENED

After hashing it out
playing it over,
swapping shock,
and issuing another collective sigh
of disappointment,
here we are
none the wiser
and none the happier
but let's do it again
next week.

LULLABY

I will not hush you, child.
I will not shame you.

I will not purse my lips
and look over your head
to the vision
of the version of you
I might have made
if it were up to me.

Only you
know the true nature
of the unpaved
paths you take
and sometimes mistake
for the way through.

You are not forgotten.
You are not a failure.
You cannot lose my love.

Stay.
Here is someone
who trusts you with your life
and still comes when you call
in the night
for a ride home.

MY BOY

He comes by
    to do laundry
        and crosses the living room
            to wrap his mother
        in his bare arms–
    his mother
        who is happy to see him
            walk through the door
                who still calls him "buddy"
            who hasn't given him up
                but leaves love notes
            in his duffle bag
        that smells like guns
            and weed
                and clean socks.

HOWARD AND WILMA

Grandpa and Grandma took me
with them to see the Passion Play.
I got to ride on the tour bus
and sleep on the floor of their hotel room
in Oberammergau where the restaurants
and guest houses are painted like Easter Eggs.

At college, forty-five minutes from their home
in Beech Grove, I sometimes called, asked them
to come get me. They always did.
We would spend the weekend being quiet
together, as they went about their chores and I
left textbooks in my backpack and played piano
or read novels. We passed Grandma's homegrown green beans
and Grandpa's pile of buttered bread inside the yellow
walls of the kitchen.

Sunday morning we sat on a wooden pew
a few blocks away, singing wordy melodies from the pages
of the Disciples of Christ hymnal
before driving to the MCL cafeteria to savor gravy,
mashed potatoes and local news with their friends.

As for the conversations that passed between us
when we were alone, I cannot recall.
Only the way my name sounded when they said it.
Only the way they said yes when I called.

OLD FRIEND

Our mothers were talking
about how close we were, the two of us.
Teenagers who found each other at church
laughing and passing communion cups.

I was dreaming of course,
so our mothers were still young–
we were all young together.

I didn't want to open my eyes
and have us not be standing there
with our stories of snow days
and driving too fast after prom
in your father's BMW.

I didn't want to be far from you
who recognized me so easily
when I was young and felt
myself a foreigner
in the world.

Maybe feeling foreign
has never fully left me.
Maybe belonging with you
is the old house I keep driving past.

First love, with the kiss
of friendship you gave me
what I needed most.

BETWEEN US

We're knee-deep
in the standing water

      of your silence.

There were years
I would have trembled
and gone fetal
left dishes undone

      while I chased
          your forgiveness

taking the truth back
like bad salmon.
I would have done
all these things

      and more, but–

I am not trembling now
and nothing is taken back.

I simply tilt my head and listen
for the slightest signal–

      a sound like–

Not today, but let's try tomorrow, or–
Of course we will work this out, or–
I know your heart, but this hurts me, or–
I am a child

      afraid.

ON YOUR BIRTHDAY

I did not write or call.
but carried through town
the ache of not writing, not calling,
of trying not to love
what is loved, and always must be.

The threads between us
have snapped.
All that's left
is to let go.

But if I could have,
I might have written:

You are part of me,
permanent ink
on many of my favorite pages
and a few of the saddest.
I wish you joy.
I wish you peace.
Friendship with those
who speak your language.
Above all
may you find within yourself
the safe love
you hoped to find
with me.

WHAT SHE REMEMBERS

Not where the baking dish goes
or whether it's Tuesday or Friday.

Not that we've already talked
about the benefits of bone broth.

These she returns to the tide;
they can come or go, no matter.

She only holds onto what she prizes.
It's all she can talk about, opening her hands to us:

Have I shown you?
Have I shown you my love?

GROWING YEARS

Old, young, what does it matter?

What can be said of my body
that would be remotely true of my soul?

I was old at twenty-six,
if you mean tired, shrinking,
and unavailable for sexy dresses
or late nights on the town.

I am now fifty and not tired.

When my body was young,
I lived in my head.

Now my skin thins
while my heart grows plump and runs the show.

There is so much to love here.
And so much that tries to love me.

I am in my growing years,
savoring the golden hour.

Aging is easy; been doing it since birth.

Being alive, at any age–
Now that takes some skill.

FROM THIS DAY FORWARD

I've made a deal with my body,
and I think it's a good one.

Listen, I said,
I'm going to love you and cherish you, okay?
In sickness and health
I promise to shelter and feed you,
pamper and speak to you
with kindness.

When you talk, I will listen.
I will trust your wisdom
and believe in you even
when you want to quit.

I'll make you laugh
and stay with you while you weep.

I will call you beautiful
and encourage you to be strong.
I will never ask you to hide
or shape yourself
into somebody you're not.

It's you and me, kid.
I choose us.

All you have to do is
keep breathing.

RENAISSANCE

At fifty, I am nine again
unworried with boys
unhurried in my day
unshackled from shyness.

At fifty, I am
a lean-limbed girl
whose mind is made up
of big ideas.

At fifty, I can't be convinced
to give up again
my own ways of seeing
a world that wants only

to belong to itself
and be free.

DAUGHTER

Before your first step.
Before you learned to speak.
Before we heard you sing.
Before you were called pretty.
Before the good grades.
Before you made us laugh.
Before you beat your record.
After you quit.
Before you learned to think for yourself.
After you changed your mind.
Before you had big dreams.
After you stopped believing.
Before you got hurt.
Before you got better.
Before he loved you.
After he left.
Before you knew it.
Daughter.
You were always divine.

ANNUAL PERFORMANCE

I can't stop smiling
at the tiny tots costumed
as yellow tree stars
and trembling with excitement
against the curtain of clouds.

Ready to shine!

The chimes, too, are warming up
on Emily's porch and I watch
like a proud sister,
camera ready.

I've seen this one before.

But I know the director
and the cast
and every year
they change it up
a little.

NO ONE TELLS US

I sit at the feet
of gingko leaves
turned fire and fallen
into autumn's amber carpet
that says to us–

    Give up being soft and green;
    forget your former beauty.

        Surrender before you go
        to nature's secret:

           You get to be gold.

I KEEP COMING BACK

Tell me again, Beloved, about us.
I may have forgotten as I went about
the business of my day.

How you first fell for me,
and keep falling for me,
even when I can't bear it.

Remind me that with you
I am always
what I am.

With you
I have always been.

When my mind hid our union from me,
the world became a nightmare.

When my senses were restored,
I looked inside my body and found

the light, the breath and movement,
of your voice, the sea

that says to the small wave:
Nothing can separate us.

IN THE FIELD BEYOND THE HOUSE

I don't believe
I took the house down,
but merely stepped onto the porch
for the first time
and observed
through the window
the overhead lighting
and the hunched backs
of the disciples.

My own shoulders
were near my ears
but outside they softened.

I don't believe
in taking things down
as much as taking long walks,
so I found my way to a field
with high grass and a rosebud sky
where I was not lonely
    or afraid
as I'd been warned,
    and not so sure, as I'd tried
    so long to be.

If you see me falling upward
into the great sky that holds
    the house
    the porch
    the fields and forests
don't worry.

Like you, I am finding
something true.

PROVOCATEUR

Will you be light

if it means casting shadows
that expose the shape
of things daily looked upon
but seldom seen?

People love prophets
of the past
but who wants to be kept
from comfort?

It's easier to repeat
the story you know than to practice
a new one,
and easier to sleep

in the dark.

LAND OF THE LIVING

I see Zion
in this land of tragedy,
where the sun climbs high in the branches
beyond my window
while my hand skates across the page
and men across the street raise rooms
that will soon fill with new neighbors
who are rowdy, or kind, like Ned
from next door who meets me
outside with jumper cables.

The car won't start,
and the wars don't end.

Everyone talks
about the world burning
and I get it–of course
I get it.

But tell me about a time
when humans weren't dying young
or afraid? I'm not saying it isn't bad.
Maybe it's worse.

Just wondering
if standing around talking
about hell on earth
has ever helped anybody
see heaven.

NOTHING SHALL BE IMPOSSIBLE

Faith of a mustard seed,

> *Yes, Lord,*
> *I have that, surely.*
> *So now, let's move some mountains.*

I began with a small one.
That stuffed rabbit high on the shelf–
in the dark before sleep–

> *Float down to me now, rabbit,*
> *Float down and prove my power.*

I have seen heftier hills
step aside since then.

I still don't know
what I had to do with the moving
    or the not-moving
or how to gauge
the weight of faith.

> *But I'm sure, Lord–I had a seed.*

I'M PRAYING AGAIN, AREN'T I?

But not like before.

This time I straddle the sun
and reach inside.

This time I can't tell where you
end and I begin.

This time you do the talking
while I say mmmm, mmmm.

Or we walk along in the spacious
silence of close friends.

This time we mostly dance
and I forget to beg or worry.

This time I fall asleep
against the bare shoulder
of your heart.

THE END OF SUFFERING

Three poisons:
Greed, Hate and Confusion–

I know which one I prefer.
I know which one has brought death.

It could be the bottle was mislabeled,
but I know now what I reach for
when what I get
is not what I desire.

Awareness slows my hand.
Breathing reveals.

Three antidotes:
Generosity, Love and Wisdom–

May I find the strength
to choose the way
that leads to peace.

TO LEAVE BEHIND
A CRITICAL HEART

Everything I judge
disintegrates

        along with the love
        I mean to give.

                God, if you agree,
                help me find flaws

                        only in rooms
                        that are mine to repair.

DISARMING

Maybe you don't
have to be
a warrior
or a soldier boy.

Maybe life
doesn't require
stealth weapons
and hard armor.

What would happen
if you let yourself
be caught
unmasked?

What if you
showed
those you fear
the face of God?

I'VE HEARD IT SAID

The Source of All Life
remembers Itself
through me.

And not only me
but also the coneflower
and the crepe myrtle,
the howling dog
and the possum prowling
the dark yard.

Someone sees you,
and sees the world
through your blinking eyes.

Someone felt your lashes fill
with saltwater
when you got the news
and watched your hands
wash each other
slowly.

Someone seeks to feel
this fragile grandeur from every angle–

Our Maker
in the darkroom of the universe
laying negatives into liquid
to raise likeness upon likeness,
no two alike.

Is it true? I don't know.

But it's a good story,
isn't it?

THREE PORTALS

Through the doorway of joy
  we welcome God

       into our arms.

Through the doorway of grief
  we welcome God

       into our hearts.

Through the doorway of compassion
  we welcome the world

       into God.

LIFE ITSELF

You are the rainy day
I've waited for.
The autumn I've just
begun to love.

You are the face
that keeps changing
without aging.

The holy soil
beneath my feet
and the song of a thousand birds
playing through my veins.

You are the voice I cherish
in the dark, the friend
who won't quit whispering
while I try to sleep.

You are the sun's mouth
kissing me awake,
the dancer dancing me
with joy

and the rose opening,
releasing me to be

fragrant.

DISCIPLE

Great Spirit, give credit
for my questions.
Collect my doubts as an offering.
You never met a more earnest
student of your love
and goodness.

I thank you
that despite man's best efforts
to make the Way straight
and systematic, you yourself never
asked me to minimize
the mystery of our Being.

When I was small, you met me
in my longing. With songs
and laughter you led
a caravan of curiosity
and I followed along
smacking the tambourine.

We spoke then–and now–in tongues
of children and mystics
beyond the borders
of the rational
or religious.

To be heard without shouting.
To be loved without condition.
To be held within my body.

These you have taught me well
and need no unlearning.

A SAFE HOUSE

She lived in a house of trembling knees
and flushed cheeks.
Her body was no sanctuary.

At any moment she could be consumed.
At any moment the possibility of pain.
At any moment all could be lost.

How then did she find this Love
that swells and fills her so that fear
has no elbow room?

I will tell you, Beloved.

Every morning she opens swollen eyes
and says to Life:

> *I am afraid.*
> *Where can I go to be safe?*

And Life responds:

> *Let's start Here.*

THANK YOU

As I recently sat lamenting not being further along in some of my creative and vocational pursuits, it dawned on me that these six years since my separation have seen the release of three studio albums, the publication of three small books (including this one), the launch of a nine-month long Creative Mastermind program and a number of retreats, in person and online. My children and I also moved three times, two graduated from high school and two from college. Suffice to say, it's been a full season of life.

Why do I say all that? To point to *the power of community* to pave a road where there isn't one.

I have done nothing at all by myself.

Not one single thing.

The contributions made by family, friends, Patrons, and Kickstarters to my work and my family's well-being are too many to count. The deep impact of your love is beyond measure.

With pleasure, I will continue wearing God out giving thanks for you.

ABOUT THE AUTHOR

Christa Wells is an award-winning songwriter, singer and speaker in Nashville, Tennessee. She co-founded and directs **ARTIST AND**, a community which empowers artists of all kinds connect and pursue their creative passions. Following her divorce in 2018, Christa began writing and speaking about resilience and her journey through grief and has released three albums of music since then (*Velveteen*, *Pacific*, and *Redwood*). She also published a book of poetry called ***BELOVED*** and a book of prose called ***BEFORE IT GETS LIGHTER***.